MW01049380

Eating Clean

Reset Your Body, Reduce Weight and Get Rid of Inflammation – Healthy Whole Food Recipes

Contents

Book Description

We all get excited when a new food outlet opens up in the neighborhood and we start making plans to visit it in no time. But have we ever ponder that is it all worth eating just every day? All those junk stuff with hot sauces artificially preserved and made? Does 'clean eating' refer to eating in expensive hotels? Does clean eating include a clean place to sit and eat? Well! Nothing of such, clean eating refers to the clean and hygienic food with the least artificial additives added to it. Let's not run behind the bush, clean eating is eating mindfully the food which will keep you healthy in the long run rather fill your stomach for the time being. Clean eating refers to eating fresh fruits, vegetables, cereals, and meat. The food should not only be clean but cooked well at home with variety and combinations, to keep your body healthy and fine.

Clean eating is eating the 'real food' in short, which has all the natural contents. The real food is minimally processed, refined and natural. Seeing the current time, our daily routine schedules have gone so busy that we have ignored ourselves on the eating habits. Grabbing food while rushing to the office, starting the day with coffee, eating pizza at lunch and steak for dinner is not what you call good hygienic eating habits.

This book credibly enhances the meaning and value of eating clean food, and how can one get started to it. Many of us know what clean eating is and want to change their lifestyle, but they do not know from where to start. This book is the perfect remedy for all such starters. It is a complete package of recipes, which will encourage you to eat healthy with variety. This book has segmented portions and it solves your hurdle of a three-day meal. The recipes are divided into breakfast, lunch and dinner. Not only this, dessert recipes are also available, which can add glimmer to your menu with least sweetened preservatives.

So follow the recipes and start hygienic and real food cooking at home. Change your lifestyle in the best healthy way. Try best not to use canned meat or seafood, look for the supermarkets where they are present in their fresh natural form. This book not only contains recipes but also the instructions to maintain the healthy diet with controlled calories. If you are going to gym or doing workouts, cut off the unnatural preservative protein drinks and follow the natural protein diet through our easy-to-make healthy recipes.
So without a delay, flip the pages and take a start to a healthy journey of a good diet! Happy cooking!

Introduction

A healthy lifestyle is an essential thing to cope up with the competitive world today, but how can you achieve it? Look around at your current lifestyle and analyze your eating habits. Starting from the morning, we take cornflakes, doughnuts, coffee, and tea. Let's look at our afternoons and evenings, the majority of us do not eat proper meals in these times due to office routine and if we do, we prefer pizza, burgers, and lasagna the most. And what about our dinners? We hardly cook at home and roam around to the restaurants looking for steaks and junk food. Now think about the originality of all the mentioned food we all tend to eat in our daily routines. Are they all natural or artificially processed? It's all artificially processed loaded with chemicals and artificial flavors. When all the meals are artificial and factory processed then how can you even imagine to stay healthy without a disease?

But it is never too late to change your eating habits and start living a new healthy life. Eating healthy does not mean the well-packed food in good packing, but it refers to the naturally processed food with original flavor and content. Clean eating refers to fresh fruits, vegetables, meat, seafood, and cereals. They keep your body naturally fit and healthy without any side effect. Fruits and vegetables play a vital role in providing enough amount of vitamins, mineral and fiber, whereas meat and sea food helps in building your protein level naturally, without making you addicted to the artificially made protein packs available in the market.

This Book completely explains in detail all the clean and easy-to-make recipes for breakfast, lunch, and dinner, which boosts up your immune system and maintains your good health in the long run. Instead of hitting the gym with preservative diet, follow it with these natural foods and build your stamina naturally. According to a research, people who tend to stick to simple and fresh diet live longer than those who bread themselves on junk and artificially processed food at large. Junk food damages liver, kidney, and stomach in the long run because of its strong chemicals.

These recipes are full of nutritional values with the least to zero artificial additives, which will take your health to betterment. Combinational food recipes of smoothies, omelets, milkshakes, meat gravies, and desserts will not only give you variety but also

Chapter 1 – Fundamentals of Clean Eating

With the passing time, the habits of clean eating are declining in the majority of us, which is leading to minor and major problems like gastric issues, cholesterol problem, obesity, kidney issues and an overall failure in the immune system. Today doctors are conducting numerous campaigns, health seminars, nutritional programs, and workshops to educate the people about clean and healthy eating, to increase the quality of life.

In today's time where everyone is sternly busy with their career oriented routines and social circles, the majority of us have forgotten the real value of 'clean eating'. With the increased tourism, vocational tours, hoteling's and social gatherings, we have started relying badly on just the readymade super mart's or hotel's food to satisfy our taste buds. Not all places maintain the level of hygiene our body needs, which is the main reason we fell ill often without getting to know the major reason.

What is Clean Eating?

Clean eating doesn't mean that the crockery or the cutlery you use should be clean or the place where you sit should be clean, yes no doubt all these things should be clean but the food you are eating should be clean in its properties. 'Clean Food' comprises of good organic diet like fresh fruits, vegetables, naturally processed dairy products, meat, seafood and whole grains. Not only this but healthy oils also very much essential for a good clean diet. Clean eating or clean food means the food which contains the least artificially processed materials and chemicals which are a loss to the body.

This book is the best source of information for those who want to change their eating habits and learn how to easily get accessible to the clean and healthy eating. So what are you waiting for, let's look down to the most important fundamentals of clean eating. Follow the following points and boost your immunity level with fresh and healthy eating habits.

✓ Limit the consumption of Processed Food

Today we eat just everything artificial, let it be the canned food, processed dairy products, sweets, chocolates, and artificially processed meat and what not. Processed food is majorly chemically composed, which is doing major harms to the body these days. Chickens are being made genetically to increase growth in the quickest time but are they healthy? No! They lack the basic nutritional composition of proteins and according to some scientists, such chickens are just machine meat, tasteless and health destructors. When you have made up your mind that you want to eat healthily and stay safe then kindly abstain from the processed food as much as possible. Look for the farm chickens and meat, go for fresh fruits and vegetables rather than the canned frozen fruits, which has been placed in the freezers since ages.

✓ Take care of Sodium

The intake of sodium in the right quantity is very much essential to maintain the healthy mineral composition of the body. Americans tend to take a lower level of sodium than required by the body and American Africans take higher than required, which has led them to fall for the diseases like high blood pressure, kidney disease, and diabetes. Be very cautious to take the right quantity to maintain robustness of the body. Avoid using readymade marinating of meat for they contain a higher level of sodium which is not beneficial for the health. Instead, do your own cooking at home in the hygienic and clean environment. When you cook from the scratch, you have all control over the spices and can adjust to them easily. Limit the high intake of salt for it can decline your good health in the worst ways.

✓ Eat Less Meat

Though meat is very much good for health and the main source of proteins, vitamin B12, and iron, but make sure you eat the ones which are not artificially processed. Too much meat in the diet is also not good for it gives a heavy feeling and it can lead to high cholesterol, high blood pressure and heart risk glitches. Try the raw form like steaks, instead eat the smaller quantity with vegetable seasonings cooked in healthy oils.

✓ Vegetables are the best!

Nothing is more fresh and best than the fresh vegetables which are rich in fiber, vitamins, and minerals. Proper intake of fresh vegetables has cured major diseases like cancer even. Vegetables can be consumed in the variety of ways like salad seasoning, pickling, and in proper meals as well. Each vegetable has its own benefit to the body and it is best to consume them fresh and of the season.

✓ Go For Whole Grains

Whole grains are very much needed by the body and must be taken in the adequate amount. Rice dishes are the most famous nowadays and they are more hygienic if cooked at home with vegetables or meat. Wheat has the benefit of cutting down excessive fat from the body, so eat wheat to stay healthy and slim naturally. According to a survey people who eat 3 or more servings of the whole grain tend to have a lower body mass index and lesser belly fat than those eating fewer servings.

Clean eating is not only beneficial for oneself but it does wonders to the family system. When you cook good healthy food in the family, you maintain health and hygiene, contributing best to your family. A happy family is always a healthy family with the least health problems and greater fitness with the longevity of life. So who would not love to see their grandparents, parents and children all happy and fit? So stick to the guidelines provided in the book and maintain your happy environment at home.
So flip on to the next chapter and see how to get started with the clean eating.

.

Chapter 2 – Getting Started with Clean Eating

We all by now know what's clean eating and what's a clean food, but do we know how to start putting it into our daily routine to stay healthy? At this point, we stuck that 'when' and 'how' to start to change our eating habits. We all need a moral and guiding boost to get started. As said old habits die hard, this is very much true with the food as well. First, train your mind and make it accept that from now onwards you have to comply with the instructions and follow it for your betterment. Most of the people start the diet with a boost but leave it in the middle because they can't comply with it for a longer period of time due to the rigid old habits made in the younger age. Consistency is very much necessary, so prepare your mind and heart first and then start the process of transformation.
The below-mentioned steps are very much useful for a robust lifestyle! Follow them and get benefitted at large.

1. Stick to the rules of 'Clean Eating'!

Like every destination has a certain path and rules to follow, likewise, the clean eating also has a definite pattern of rules to follow, then only one can attain the healthy destination.

- Skip White: skip sugar and white flour initially for it leaves a drastic effect on the body. Sugar is a slow poison for the body which makes the body addicted for itself to destroy it at its best. All the white things are artificially processed with loads of artificial materials and chemicals, which are becoming one of the main reason diabetes in people.

- No Alcohol: Alcohol is the worst thing to your body for it destroys your every part of the body leaving you empty all inside. Never do the mistake of adding wine to your fresh food cooking for it destroys their freshness and instead contaminates them with its filthy properties.

- Take Healthy sources of Fats: Make sure that the fats you are consuming are from the healthy sources. Use healthy oils like olive oils, nut oils, and coconut oils. Mae a habit of cooking food in olive oil.

- Take fresh vegetables, fruits, and meat: when you go for shopping always look for the fresh vegetables and fruits. Fresh things contain most of the vitamins, fibers, and minerals. To maintain a healthy diet eat combinations of meat with vegetables for lunch and dinner.

2. Give yourself treat as well:

I know it's difficult to stick to the new diet consistently for a longer period of time and there ought to be a day where you can treat yourself with whatever you want to eat. But make sure you don't make that treat day just the every alternate day to your new diet. Fix it once a day, maybe a Saturday and enjoy the meals you love and satisfy your old habits by dining out with you family and friends. Too much self-restriction at times deviates you from your real goal.

3. Clean your fridge first!

Before you think to start the healthy cooking, make sure your fridge is clean enough to keep the fresh edibles. A clean fridge is very much necessary and if it's not properly cleaned the fungus and bacteria multiplies at large contaminating your food as soon as they are placed into it. So take a day spare and clean the fridge with the minutest detail and then place the things into it.

4. Clean your Kitchen Cabinets, Desk, and floor:

For a healthy cooking, the place where the cooking is meant to take place should be clean enough as well. Make sure you clean the kitchen, wipe the floors well to remove bacteria, clean the cabinets and clean the kitchen dustbin, all on the regular basis. If the kitchen is not kept clean then germs from the surroundings can easily rest on your food and make you ill at health.

5. Prepare your Grocery List

When you have finally planned to change your old routine, it is very much essential to keep your mind clear of the food item you will be requiring to cook and eat. Make a list of the grocery items and make sure you don't buy the fresh fruits and vegetables in bulk for they get soft in the fridge even, if kept for a longer period of time. Buy the fresh stock of vegetables and fruits weekly in order to maintain their nutritional value alive. Meat is not an issue for it can be kept in stock in the freezer but fruits and vegetables don't stay fresh even in the fridge for long.

6. Schedule your Cooking time

The majority of us are busy with our jobs, kids, and many other engagements so it's very much important to fix your time to step in the kitchen and start your healthy cooking. Fix the time so you do not mess up with the schedule set. Once you have made the food, make sure to clean the dustbin and store the cooked meal well. You can always take out time to prepare things in advance. For e.g.: if you want to make pickled fruits and vegetables, or canned food, or jams and marmalades, then take out time at the weekend and stock them. You will be free from any sort of stress for weeks or so.

7. **Schedule your Menu:**

Fix days for different meals to get the variety of nutrition. Make a menu that on which day you will cook what ad stick it to your fridge, so in case if you have anything less for that dish, you can easily buy it before time. Scheduling menu can save you from the confusions of what to cook each day. A balanced diet is very much necessary and by dividing it per day can make it very easy for you to remember what to make when, and your body would get used to it in a passage of time.

These are very easy steps to follow for a healthy diet plan. You need to understand this as well that it takes a time to adjust to the new routine and pattern, so stay patient and follow it with positivity and enthusiasm.

Chapter 3 – Clean Eating Breakfasts

Breakfasts are very important to kick-start a healthy day and to maintain your energy level all day long. Here are some real good recipes to be followed to stay away from artificial food and add on the natural ones.

Recipe 01: Mixed Berry Cobbler Smoothie

Ingredients: *It makes the serving for one only.*

- ✓ ½ Cup almonds, hemp seed or coconut milk

- ✓ ½ Cup strawberries (fresh or frozen)

- ✓ ½ cup blueberries (fresh or frozen)

- ✓ ½ Cup blackberries

- ✓ 2 or 3 dates

Method: Take a clean blender and insert all the ingredients into it. Now blend them all together and make a fine smoothie. This smoothie is all natural and does not contain any preservative, so add it to your clean eating breakfast list to stay healthy and active all day.

Recipe 02: Peach Milkshake

Milkshakes have always been famous for providing the best nutritional values in the morning. Milkshakes are good no matter which ever the fruit is. According to a research if two tablespoons of coconut oil are added to it then it will be ideal to consume for coconut oil increases the metabolism at large.

Ingredients:

- ✓ 1 Cup almonds or hemp seed milk
- ✓ 1 Cup peaches (fresh or frozen)
- ✓ ½ Cup Pineapple Juice (Fresh)
- ✓ ½ Cup banana (frozen)
- ✓ 1 tsp. Coconut Oil

Method: In a clean dry blender, insert all the ingredients and blend it well. Blend it until it forms a fine smooth milkshake. It is all your choice whether to take it alone or with sandwiches.

Recipe 03: Banana and Coconut Water

Banana and Coconut water, what an amalgamation of a healthy doze! In this recipe, we have used avocado, and hemp seeds, which are the main source of proteins and add great benefit to your overall diet. In this smoothie, we have also used cacao nibs and wheatgrass, which play a vital role in the provision of magnesium to the body. Magnesium is the very important element to maintain energy level, especially in athletes. So if you are an athlete or do regular workouts then you surely must add this to your breakfast menu list.

Ingredients:

✓ 1/2 Cup Banana (chopped and frozen)

✓ 1 small handful spinach

✓ ¼ ripe avocado (pitted)

✓ 1 handful berries (frozen)

✓ 1 ½ tsp. shelled hemp seeds

✓ 1 tbsp. raw cacao nibs

✓ ¼ tsp. wheatgrass powder

✓ ¼ cucumber (chopped)

✓ 1 cup coconut oil water

Method: Before putting all the ingredients in the blender, make sure the bananas are frozen and in solid form. Before making the smoothie, freeze bananas and add them solid in the blender along with the other ingredients. Mix them well until a smooth texture is formed. If you find the texture very thick, add a little water to it and have it early in the morning.

Recipe 04: Healthy Quinoa Pancakes

A healthy breakfast does require a little effort to be made but it does wonder to your body later. Quinoa pancakes are the best source of gluten-free breakfast, packed with proteins, a perfect thing to start a fresh day. Is not only good to be used for breakfast but it can also be eaten in the lunch time. When you are using quinoa, remember to soak it overnight. Always go for this recipe whenever you feel like eating a healthy meal with the best taste!

Ingredients:

- ✓   ½ Cup Quinoa

- ✓   ½ Cup water

- ✓   1 tsp. salt

- ✓   Coconut Oil

- ✓   Maple Syrup (for topping)

Method:

- Soak the Quinoa overnight by taking a large bowl and placing quinoa in it along with 4 cups of water. You need to soak it for at least 8 hours. Once the time is complete, drain and rinse it. Stir quinoa in salt and add it to blender.

- In the blender now add ½ cup water and 1 teaspoon of salt, and grind. Make sure the batter made is not too thick or too thin. The consistency should be moderate. If it's too thick, add water, and if it is too thin then add quinoa.

- Take coconut oil and heat it over medium heat in a large pan. In the heated oil, add ¼ cup of batter and cook for around ½ minutes till the bubbles appear and the corners turn golden brown.

- Turn over the pancake side and cook for another minute. Make sure both the sides are well made. Remove from the stove and serve with maple syrup, fruit topping, honey, cream or anything of your choice.

Recipe 05: Huevos Rancheros Breakfast Sandwich

Ingredients:

- ✓ 2 Muffins (halved and toasted)
- ✓ 1/3 Cup of refined beans
- ✓ 2 eggs
- ✓ Salsa
- ✓ Salt
- ✓ Pepper
- ✓ 1 ripple Avocado

Method:

- • Take 2 muffins, half and toast them, meanwhile peel Avocado and mash it with the help of the fork.

Once it's done, add salt to taste to it and heat beans till they get warm. Spread the bean mixture on the bottom of the muffins and spread avocado on the top of the muffin.

- Heat a pan over medium heat, grease it with olive oil and crack 2 eggs into the pan. Add eggs one at a time, sprinkle salt and taste unto it according to your taste. Cook for 1 to 2 minutes, flip the sides of the eggs carefully and season again with salt and pepper.
- Place the cooked eggs on the top of the muffin, add salsa on the top and place avocado on top to serve best.

Recipe 06: Marinara-Poached eggs

Ingredients:
- ✓ Olive Oil

- ✓ ¼ Yellow Onion

- ✓ Red pepper

- ✓ ½ Cup Marinara Sauce

Method:
- Take a pan, heat 2 tsp. of olive oil in it over medium flame and add ¼ of small yellow onion until it gets brown. Add a pinch of red pepper to it and ½ a cup of marinara sauce.

- Heat the sauce for a minute and add one egg into it. Now cover the pan and rubble over low heat for around 7 minutes.

- Serve the poached eggs with wheat pita bread or with any bread of your choice.

Recipe 07: Spinach Omelet

Ingredients:

✓ 1 tsp. Canola Oil

✓ 1 egg

✓ Baby Spinach (1 cup)

✓ 1 tbsp. goat cheese (crumbled)

Method:

- Take a non-stick pan and add 1 tsp. of canola oil and heat it on medium flame.

- Take 1 egg and add it to the pan and spin it. Cook it for around 1 minute.

- Sauté 1 cup of baby spinach in the same pan for 1 minute again.

- Pour 1 tsp. of oil on the egg along with the 1 tsp. Of goat cheese.

- Garnish it with baby spinach, roll it up, cut into half and have this nutritional breakfast often in your menu list.

- This healthy breakfast provides 2 grams of carbohydrates, 17 grams of fat, 198 calories, 1 gram of fiber and 301mg of sodium.

Recipe 08: Tex-Mex Scrambled Eggs

Ingredients:
- ✓ 1 tsp. Corn tortilla
- ✓ 1/8 Jalapeno
- ✓ ¼ red bell pepper (diced)
- ✓ 2 eggs
- ✓ ¼ green bell pepper
- ✓ 1 tbsp. cheddar cheese
- ✓ 1 tbsp. cilantro (chopped)
- ✓ Onion
- ✓ tomato

Method:
- Take a small skillet and add 1 teaspoon of canola oil to it and heat it.
- Add a corn tortilla and pan fry it for 2 minutes each side. Remove it from heat and dice it.
- In the same pan sauté jalapeno, red bell pepper, onion, tomato and green bell pepper.

- Now whisk two eggs and add them to the pan along with vegetables. Stir it in the tortilla and add 1 tsp. of cheddar cheese along with 1 tbsp. of chopped cilantro.

- This healthy nutritious breakfast comprises of 308 calories, 21 grams of carbohydrates, 17 grams of fat, 17 grams of protein, 4 grams of fiber and 203 mg sodium.

Recipe 09: Creamy Vanilla Breakfast Pudding

Ingredients:
- ✓ Rice cereal
- ✓ 1 egg
- ✓ ¼ tsp. vanilla extract
- ✓ ¼ tsp. cinnamon
- ✓ 1 tsp. sugar

✓ 2 tbsp. peach (chopped)

✓ ¼ tsp. cinnamon

Method:

- Take a small bowl, whisk an egg into it, prepare rice cereal seeing the package directions but do not add salt and add it to the saucepan.

- Whisk egg and cereal to make a mixture and add ¼ tsp. of vanilla extract, 1 tsp. sugar and ¼ tsp. of cinnamon. Simmer the mixture for 2 minutes and do the topping with chopped peach.

Recipe 10: Easy Cheesy Baked Eggs

Ingredients:

✓ 1 tsp. whole milk

✓ ¼ tsp. butter

✓ 1 tsp. parmesan (grated)

✓ 1 egg

- ✓ 1 tbsp. tomato (chopped)
- ✓ 1 tsp. chives (chopped)
- ✓ Muffin

Method:
- In a pan add 1 tsp. whole milk, 1 tsp. parmesan, ¼ tsp. butter and boil it for 2 minutes until the bubble appears.

- Add egg to the pan and add tomato in chopped form from the top. Broil it for 7 minutes and set it aside for 2 minutes.

- Scatter 1 tsp. of chive and serve or have it with whole grain muffin for best taste.

Chapter 4 – Clean Eating Lunch Recipes

Recipe 01: Greek Salad with Pita Croutons

Ingredients:
- ✓ 1 pita (whole grain)
- ✓ 1 lemon (juiced)
- ✓ 1 tbsp. olive oil
- ✓ 1 garlic clove (minced)
- ✓ Salt and pepper (to taste)
- ✓ 3 cups romaine lettuce (chopped) mixed with cucumbers, tomatoes, and red bell pepper
- ✓ 2 tbsp. reduced-fat feta cheese
- ✓ 1/2 cup canned chickpeas, rinsed & drained
- ✓ 2 tbsp. olives (chopped)

Method:
- Toast the pita whole-grain until it becomes crunchy and chop it into cubes.

- In a bowl take lemon juice, oil, garlic, salt, and pepper and whisk together.

- Mix all the ingredients and toss lemon dressing with the rest of the ingredients, including the pita pieces.

Recipe 02: Rosemary & Zucchini Flatbread

Ingredients:

- ✓ 1 flatbread (whole grain)

- ✓ ½ cup zucchini

- ✓ ¼ cup mozzarella

- ✓ 1 tsp. rosemary (dried)

- ✓ 1 cup grapes (halved)

- ✓ 2 tbsp. almonds (sliced)

Method:

- ✓ Preheat the oven to 350 degrees F and heat the flatbread on the baking sheet for around 7 minutes.

- ✓ Remove the baking tray from the oven and top with 1/2 cup thinly sliced zucchini, 1/4 cup grated mozzarella (partly skimmed), and 1 tsp. dried rosemary. Bake it for around 7 minutes until cheese is melted.

- ✓ Now mix 1 cup of grapes with almonds. Serve at room temperature with the grape salad.

Recipe 03: Thai Shrimp Po' Boy

Ingredients:
- ✓ Shrimp (2 ounces)

- ✓ 2 tsp. Chilli garlic sauce

- ✓ 3 tbsp. avocado (chopped)

- ✓ ¼ cup carrots (shredded)

- ✓ 2 tbsp. cilantro (chopped)

- ✓ 1 tbsp. lime juice

- ✓ ¼ cup cucumber (sliced)

Method:
- ✓ Take 2 ounces of shrimps (cooked and tails removed), and cook them with 2 tsp. of chili garlic sauce.

- ✓ Slice the whole-grain roll lengthwise and fill it with shrimps, 3 tbsp. sliced or chopped avocado, ¼ cup sliced cucumber, and ¼ cup shredded carrots.

- ✓ Use 2 tbsp. of cilantro and 1 tbsp. of fresh lime juice as topping and serve.

Recipe 04: Mediterranean Pasta Salad with Tuna

Ingredients:
- ✓ 1 ½ ounces pasta (whole grain)

- ✓ 3 ounces tune

- ✓ ½ cup grape (halved)

- ✓ Tomatoes

- ✓ ½ cup artichokes (drained and quartered)

- ✓ 3 tbsp. black olives (sliced and pitted)

- ✓ 1 tbsp. fresh lime juice

- ✓ 2 tsp. olive oil

- ✓ Salt & pepper (to taste)

Method:
- ✓ Cook pasta in hot water, drain out and set cool.

- ✓ Take all the ingredients and mix well with pasta.

- ✓ Add salt and pepper to taste for sprinkling before serving.

Recipe 05: Slow Cooker Savory Soup

Ingredients:
- ✓ 2 cups carrots (sliced)

- ✓ 1 large sweet potato (cut into 1/2" cubes)

- ✓ 1 cup fresh green beans (or frozen)

- ✓ 1/2 cup fresh cilantro (chopped)

- ✓ 1 small onion (diced)

- ✓ 1 clove garlic (minced)

- ✓ 2 (15 ounces) cans black beans (drained and rinsed)

- ✓ ½ tsp. crushed red pepper flakes

- ✓ ½ tsp. black pepper

- ✓ 1 tsp. chili powder

- ✓ 1 tsp. cumin

- ✓ Kosher or sea salt (to taste)

- ✓ 2 cups vegetable juice

- ✓ 2 cups vegetable broth (low-sodium)

Method:

- Combine all ingredients in the slow cooker, cover and cook on low for around 6-8 hours, or until veggies get tender. Now add 1 tbsp. of cheddar cheese, depending on your taste.

- Sauté onion in 1 tbsp. of olive oil for around 5 minutes until it gets tender. Add garlic to it and insert in the slow cooker along with other ingredients.

- You can also add 2 cups of coarsely chopped kale at last minute of cooking.

Recipe 06: Spinach & Bean Burrito Wrap

Ingredients:
- ✓ 6 cups baby spinach (loosely packed)

- ✓ 1 (15 ounces) can black beans (rinsed & drained)

- ✓ 1 ½ cups brown rice or Mexican Rice (cooked)

- ✓ ½ cup romaine heart lettuce (chopped)

- ✓ ½ cup cheddar cheese, reduced-fat (grated)

- ✓ ½ cup Salsa

- ✓ 6 tbsp. Greek yogurt (fat-free)

- ✓ Kosher or sea salt (to taste)

- ✓ 6 (8" whole grain) wraps (or tortillas)

Method:
- Preheat oven to 300 degrees and warm tortillas in them.

- In a food processor chop spinach and heat it on medium heat in a large skillet for around 3 minutes.

34

- Distribute spinach and bean mixture in the middle of the wrappings and add ¼ cup of rice to each wrapping. Now add lettuce, salsa, cheese and Greek yogurt over the wrappings.

- Fold the wraps well and serve.

Recipe 07: Quinoa and Vegetable Stir-Fry

Ingredients:
- ✓ 1 cup pre-rinsed quinoa

- ✓ 2 cups vegetable broth (optional chicken broth)

- ✓ 1 tbsp. olive oil

- ✓ 1 tsp. sesame seed oil

- ✓ 1 cup carrots (finely diced)

- ✓ ½ cup green onions (minced)

- ✓ 2 cloves garlic (minced)

- ✓ ½ cup frozen peas (thawed)

- ✓ 2 eggs (beaten)

- ✓ Kosher or sea salt (to taste)

- ✓ 2 tbsp. Soy Sauce

Method:
- In a saucepan add quinoa and broth and bring it to the boil. When the boil reaches, reduce the heat to simmer and cook for 15 minutes until the liquid has been absorbed. When the

quinoa has been heated, keep it aside to cool. Refrigerate for around two hours and then stir-fry.

- Take a large skillet, heat it on medium flame and add to it carrots, green onion, and cover it until it gets tender. Cook it for around 8 minutes and then add garlic to it.

- In a medium saucepan, add quinoa and broth, turn to medium-high heat, cover, bring to a boil and reduce heat to a simmer. Cook until all liquid has been absorbed, about 15 minutes. Remove from heat and allow to cool. Refrigerate quinoa until cold, approximately two hours. Save time by cooking ahead and make the stir-fry the next day. Add peas and quinoa and cook it for another 6 minutes.

- You can also add eggs if you wish to. If you are adding eggs then push quinoa to the sides of the skillet and add eggs to it and scramble.

- Scramble the eggs and stir well. Add Soya sauce and cook it for a minute before serving.

Chapter 5 – Clean Eating Dinner Recipes

Recipe 01: Arugula, Grape, and Sunflower Seed Salad

Ingredients:
- ✓ 3 tbsp. vinegar
- ✓ 1 tsp. honey
- ✓ 1 tsp. maple syrup
- ✓ ½ tsp. mustard (stone-ground)
- ✓ 2 tsp. grapeseed oil

- ✓ 7 cups baby arugula (loosely packed)
- ✓ 2 cups red grapes (halved)
- ✓ 2 tbsp. sunflower seed kernels (toasted)
- ✓ 1 tsp. fresh thyme (chopped)
- ✓ ¼ tsp salt
- ✓ ¼ tsp black pepper (freshly ground)

Method:

- In a bowl combine vinegar, syrup, honey, and mustard and gradually add oil and whisk.

- Take a large bowl, Syndicate arugula, grapes, seeds, and thyme. Drizzle vinegar mixture over arugula; sprinkle with salt and pepper and toss gently to coat.

Recipe 02: Vegetable Hash with Poached Eggs

Ingredients:

- ✓ 4 tsp. olive oil

- ✓ 1 cup Vidalia (chopped)

- ✓ 1 cup (1/4-inch-thick) small red potatoes

- ✓ 1 tsp. dried herbes

- ✓ 1 cup zucchini (diced)

- ✓ 1 cup yellow squash (diced)

- ✓ 1 cup green beans (trimmed and cut into 1/2-inch pieces)

- ✓ ½ tsp. kosher salt

- ✓ ½ teaspoon freshly ground black pepper (divided)

- ✓ 2 cups seeded tomato (chopped)

- ✓ 2 tbsp.chives (thinly sliced)

- ✓ 2 tbsp. fresh flat-leaf parsley (chopped)

✓ 1 tbsp. white vinegar

✓ 4 eggs (large)

✓ 1 ounce Parmesan cheese (shredded , about 1/4 cup)

Method:

- Take a large nonstick skillet and heat over medium-high heat and add oil. Now add onion, potatoes, and herbes de Provence; spread mixture in a single layer in pan. Cook for around 4 minutes, without stirring, or until potatoes turn slightly brown,

- Now reduce heat to medium and stir in zucchini, yellow squash, beans, salt, and 3/8 tsp. pepper; cook for 3 minutes. Remove pan from heat; cover and let stand it for 5 minutes. Stir in tomato, chives, and parsley.

- Add water to the skillet, at the two-thirds level and bring it to the boil. Now reduce heat; rumble and stir in vinegar. Once the boiling part is done well, break each egg into a custard cup and gently pour eggs into the pan and cook for around 3 minutes or until it is done.

- Take 4 plates and divide the mixture evenly into them by removing the eggs carefully from the pan. Top each plate with the egg serving and sprinkle black pepper and cheeses according to your choice and preference.

Recipe 03: Oven-fried Sweet Potatoes

Ingredients:

✓ 4 medium sweet potatoes (peeled and cut into 1/4-inch slices (about 1 1/2 pounds)

✓ 1 tbsp. olive oil

✓ ¼ teaspoon salt

✓ ¼ tsp. pepper

✓ Vegetable cooking spray

✓ 1 tbsp.fresh parsley (finely chopped)

✓ 1 tsp. grated orange rind

✓ 1 small garlic clove (minced)

Method:

- In a large bowl combine sweet potatoes, pepper, salt and olive oil and toss gently for coating.

- Take a large baking sheet and assemble sweet potatoes on it and bake at 400° for almost 30 minutes. Switch the sides of the potato slices after 15 minutes.

- In a bowl add parsley, orange rind, and garlic and stir them well. Sprinkle the parsley mixture over the sweet potato slices for good garnishing.

Recipe 04: Mediterranean Stuffed Chicken Breasts

Chicken is the healthy way of increasing your protein level, and especially when it is made in the combination of red pepper, feta, and olives. It's an energy booster but makes sure your sodium and calories are under check. It is all your choice whether to grill it or sauté it with quinoa

Ingredients:

- ✓ 1 large red bell pepper
- ✓ ¼ cup (1 ounce) crumbled feta cheese
- ✓ 2 tbsp pitted kalamata olives (finely chopped)
- ✓ 1 tbsp. fresh basil (minced)
- ✓ 8 (6 ounces) skinless, boneless chicken breasts

Method:

- Take the large bell pepper and cut it lengthwise, make sure to remove its seeds. Preheat oven alongside and place the red peppers in the baking tray and broil it till it gets black.

- Prepare grill to medium heat and combine cheese, bell pepper, olive and basil together.

- Cut chicken breast in a way that it forms a pocket to get stuffed. Cut the breast horizontally from the middle but do not half it.

- Fill the pockets with bell pepper mixture, salt, and black pepper. Grill chicken and make sure to grill each side for 6 minutes or until each side is done well.

- Remove from the grill and cover it loosely with foil to serve.

Recipe 05: Peppercorn-Crusted Beef Tenderloin with Gremolata

Ingredients:

- ✓ 4 (4-ounce) beef tenderloin steaks (trimmed (about 1 inch thick)
- ✓ Cooking spray
- ✓ 2 tsp. cracked black pepper
- ✓ ½ tsp. kosher salt
- ✓ 4 tsp. canola oil
- ✓ ¼ cup fresh flat-leaf parsley (chopped)
- ✓ 3 tbsp. fresh cilantro (chopped)
- ✓ 1 ½ tsp. garlic (chopped)
- ✓ 1 teaspoon chopped fresh oregano
- ✓ ½ teaspoon grated lemon rind
- ✓ 1 tbsp. fresh lemon juice
- ✓ ¼ tsp. red pepper (crushed)

Method:

- Heat oven at medium heat and coat steaks with oil, pepper and ¼ tsp. of salt. Add the steaks to pan and cook around for 3 minutes at each side and make sure they are done well.

- Now take a small bowl and combine the remaining ingredients with 1 tbsp. of oil, parsley, and ¼ tsp. of salt.

Recipe 06: Arctic Char with Orange-Caper Relish

Ingredients:

✓ 1 cup orange sections

✓ 2 tbsp. slivered red onion

✓ 1 tbsp. fresh flat-leaf parsley (chopped)

✓ 1 tablespoon capers (minced)

- ✓ 1 tsp. grated orange rind
- ✓ 1 tbsp. fresh orange juice
- ✓ 1 tbsp. extra-virgin olive oil
- ✓ 1 tsp. rice vinegar
- ✓ 1/8 tsp. ground red pepper
- ✓ 4 (6-ounce) arctic char fillets
- ✓ ½ tsp. kosher salt
- ✓ ½ tsp. freshly ground black pepper
- ✓ Cooking spray

Method:
- From the ingredient list add first 9 ingredients to the small bowl and toss them well when all the things have been combined.

- Take a large skillet and heat it over medium heat. Take fish and sprinkle it salt and pepper and add it to the pan. Cook the fish for around 4 minutes on each side until it is done well.

- Serve this delicious dinner by placing one fillet on each plate and top it with ¼ cup of relish.

Recipe 07: Chicken Kebabs and Nectarine Salsa

Ingredients:
- ✓ 1 tbsp. brown sugar

- ✓ 1 tbsp. olive oil

- ✓ 1 tbsp. fresh lime juice

- ✓ 2 tsp. chili powder

- ✓ 1 tsp. bottled minced garlic

- ✓ ½ tsp. kosher salt

- ✓ ½ teaspoon ground cumin

- ✓ ¼ teaspoon freshly ground black pepper

- ✓ 1 ½ pounds skinless, boneless chicken breast halves, cut into 24 (2-inch) pieces

- ✓ 1 large red onion (cut into 32 (2-inch) pieces)

- ✓ Cooking spray

- ✓ 2 cups diced nectarine (about 3)

- ✓ ½ cup red bell pepper (diced)

- ✓ 1/4 cup red onion (thinly sliced)

- ✓ 2 tbsps. fresh cilantro leaves

- ✓ 1 ½ tbsp. fresh lime juice

- ✓ 2 tsp. minced seeded jalapeño pepper

- ✓ ¼ tsp. kosher salt

- ✓ ½ cup peeled avocado (diced)

Method:

- Preheat broiler and add first 9 ingredients from the ingredient list in a shallow dish and let it stand for around 15 minutes.

- Take skewers and place on the chopped onion pieces and chicken pieces. Place the skewers on the broiler pan and keep coat it well with oil.

- Lastly, combine nectarines and other 6 ingredients in a bowl and gently stir in avocado. Do add a/4 teaspoon of salt for taste.

Recipe 08: Classic Roast Chicken

Ingredients:
- ✓ 1 (4-pound) whole roasting chicken
- ✓ 2 tsp. unsalted butter (softened)
- ✓ 1 ½ tsp. fresh thyme (minced)
- ✓ 1 tsp. paprika
- ✓ 1 tsp. ground coriander
- ✓ 2 tsp. extra-virgin olive oil
- ✓ ¾ teaspoon salt
- ✓ ¼ tsp. freshly ground black pepper
- ✓ 2 garlic cloves (minced)
- ✓ 3 shallots (peeled and halved)
- ✓ 3 fresh thyme sprigs
- ✓ 1 lemon (quartered)

Method:

- Remove the extra fats from the chicken while cleaning it. Preheat oven to 350 degrees.

- Take a small bowl and combine butter with the first 7 ingredients and rub it well onto chicken.

- Place the marinated chicken on the rack in the roasting pan. Place thyme sprigs and lemon in the cavity of the chicken. Fill it for a good juicy taste.

- Place the chicken on the baking tray and bake it for 45 minutes at 35 degrees.

- Remove it when done and serve it with any sauce or French fries.

Chapter 6 – Clean Eating Snacks and Salads

Recipe 01: Skinny Peanut Butter Yogurt Dip

We all have a certain craving for a good sweet dish but how to get a clean one? Well! This recipe will provide you the best taste and nutritional value. Skinny Peanut Butter Yogurt Dip is a nutty and sweet recipe with the scrumptious yet creamy texture.

Peanut butter is rich in protien and dietary fiber and is the best way to keep your sugar level in position and satisfy your quick hunger. So follow the recipe and enjoy the best sweet side dish at home, with the clean ingredients.

Ingredients:
- ✓ ½ cup Greek yogurt (fat-free and plain)
- ✓ ¼ cup natural peanut butter (crunchy)

Method:
- In a small bowl, combine all the ingredients and refrigerate until ready to eat.

- Serve it with your favorite fruits or vegetables.

Recipe 02: Peanut Butter Banana Cups

When it comes to the healthy clean eating, the control of calories has to be done to maintain a healthy weight. But no matter what we all crave for sweet things and this recipe is the best to boost your sugar level at an instant.

In this recipe, we have combined peanut butter with the bananas to provide taste and controlled calories. Dark chocolate has been used because it is lower in sugar and rich in flavonoids and peanut butter for protein and banana for antioxidants.

Ingredients:

- ✓   ¾ cup dark chocolate chips (can also be dark chocolate cut into small pieces)

- ✓   1 banana (medium,peeled and sliced into 16 rounds)

- ✓   ¼ cup peanut butter (natural)

- ✓   1 tbsp. melted coconut oil (unrefined extra-virgin is preferred)

- ✓   16 Baking cups (1.25-inch)

Method:

- •   Take the saucepan and melt chocolate in the double boiler at low heat. Combine into it melted coconut oil and peanut butter.

- Place the sheet on the counter top and place baking cups on the top.

- Add the melted chocolate layer at the bottom of each baking cup, followed by the banana slice and 1 teaspoon of peanut butter mixture and again coat it with chocolate and freeze it for an hour.

- If the peanut butter gets soft quickly, add 1 tablespoon of powdered sugar to peanut butter and coconut oil mixture, before you add them to the baking cups.

Recipe 03: Watermelon & Cucumber Salad

When you are hungry and don't feel like having a heavy meal but still you want to end the craving, then this quick recipe will do wonders in your menu list. Watermelon with the chunks of cucumber not only kills the heat but also satisfies the hunger urge.

Ingredients:
Salad
- ✓ 4 heaping cups bite-size watermelon cubes (seedless)
- ✓ 1 large cucumber (rinsed and cut into bite-size triangles)
- ✓ ½ cup feta cheese crumbles
- ✓ 12 fresh mint leaves, sliced into ribbons"
- ✓ 3 whole mint leaves (for garnishing)

Lime Vinaigrette

- ✓ 1 tbsp. freshly squeezed lime juice (of one lime)
- ✓ ½ tbsp. extra-virgin olive oil
- ✓ 2 tsp. honey (raw preferred)
- ✓ ¼ tsp. kosher or sea salt
- ✓ ¼ tsp. black pepper

Method:

- Heap mint leaves into two piles. Slice them thin and make them into ribbons.

- Whisk together all the ingredients for dressing.

- Add dressing and salad ingredients to a serving bowl and gently toss to coat.

- Garnish with mint leaves or sprigs if preferred.

Recipe 04: 5-Ingredient Mexican Corn

Ingredients:
- ✓ 4 corns

- ✓ 1/3 cup plain Greek yogurt

- ✓ ½ cup fresh, finely grated añejo or cotija cheese (Mexican cheese) or fresh, finely grated Parmesan cheese

- ✓ 1 tbsp. chili powder

- ✓ 1 lime (cut into wedges)

- ✓ ¼ cup cilantro (finely chopped)

Method:
- Take a pot filled with water, add salt and boil it. Now add corns to it and boil for around 15 minutes until they become tender.

- Place corns on the broiler pan and broil 5 minutes.

- In a dish place the corn with Greek yogurt and sprinkle cheese, chili powder, lemon juice and cilantro on top.

- You can do the dressing of your choice, it's all up to you. Enjoy!

Recipe 05: 6-Ingredient Caprese Pasta Salad

This 6-ingredient Caprese Pasta Salad is best to satisfy your odd time hunger. Instead of eating any junk or full of calorie meal, it is always best to go for the clean option, which will not ruin your health. It's a very popular dish because it is easy to make, healthy to eat and light to the stomach. Salads are always refreshing to eat and this one will be best to be consumed in the summers for a refreshing feel. So try this simple, refreshing and nutritious recipe and enjoy it with your family!

Ingredients:
- ✓ 4 cups cooked whole grain pasta
- ✓ 1 (8-ounce) fresh mozzarella ball (diced)
- ✓ 8 Roma tomatoes or 12 cherry tomatoes (sliced in half)
- ✓ 10 fresh basil leaves (roughly chopped)
- ✓ ¼ cup Extra-virgin olive oil

✓ Sea salt (to taste)

Method:
- Boil the pasta and set it aside to cool.

- Take a bowl and combine all the ingredients.

- Toss well to combine and serve!

Recipe 06: Turkey Sausage Balls

Turkish Sausage Balls can be eaten in the dinner as well as for the side dish. There are a variety of recipes to try it with. You can have it with speggetis or rice or any gravy of your choice, for cooking is all about creatively playing with your taste buds.

It can be consumed as an appetizer or as a proper meal, the choice is all yours. These meatballs are nothing but the small packages of protein doze, which are very much essential to keep your immunity active naturally.

Ingredients:

- ✓ 1 pound turkey (lean ground)
- ✓ 1 tsp. ground fennel seeds
- ✓ 1 tsp. dried oregano
- ✓ ½ tsp. crushed red pepper flakes
- ✓ ½ tsp. kosher or salt
- ✓ ¼ tsp. black pepper
- ✓ 2 tbsp. olive oil

Method:
- In a large bowl, mix all the ingredients and shape them into balls.

- Take a pan, add oil and heat it on medium flame. Place the meatballs in batches and cook them until they no more remain raw and changes color to a beautiful brown.

- Cook them for around 8 minutes, after the making process is done, place them on the tissue paper and let the tissue drain its extra oil. Cover them to keep warm.

- When all the batches are made, serve them either with any sauce or pasta or rice. The choice is all yours.

Recipe 07: No-Mayo Chicken Salad

Ingredients

- ✓ 1 pound chicken breast (cut into bite size pieces)

- ✓ ¼ cup extra-virgin olive oil

- ✓ 3 tbsp. lemon juice

- ✓ ¼ tsp. kosher or sea salt

- ✓ ¼ tsp. black pepper

- ✓ 1 cup cherry tomatoes (halved or quartered)

- ✓ ½ cup diced celery

- ✓ 1 tbsp. freshly chopped dill (or 1 teaspoon dried)

- ✓ ¼ cup freshly chopped parsley

- ✓ 6 large lettuce leaves (for serving)

Method:

- Take a large skillet, add 1 tbsp. of olive oil and heat it on medium flame. Add chicken to it and sauté it until it turns color to golden brown.

- In a bowl, add lemon juice, salt, pepper and olive oil and once the chicken has been cooked, add it to the bowl and toss it in tomatoes, parsley, celery, and dill.

- Garnish this delicious salad with lettuce leaves and serve!

Chapter 7: Clean Eating Desserts

Recipe 01: Black Forest Banana Split

Ingredients:
- ✓ 2 cups nonfat ricotta cheese

- ✓ 2 bananas (split lengthwise)

- ✓ 16 walnut (halves)

- ✓ 1 tsp. cocoa powder (unsweetened)

- ✓ 2 tsp. cherry (concentrate)

Method:
- Spoon ricotta cheese into a dessert dish and place a banana half on each side of the cheese.

- Place the walnut halves on top of the bananas and dust with the cocoa powder.

- Sprinkle the cherry concentrate on top and serve. These ingredients make two servings. For more servings, increase the quantity.

- Its nutritional facts are as follows: 377 calories, 23g protein, 40g carbohydrate, 11g fat and 3.5g fiber

Recipe 02: Greek Yogurt with Oranges and Mint

Ingredients:
- ✓ 6 tbsp. Greek yogurt (fat-free)

- ✓ 1 1/2 tsp. honey

- ✓ 1 large orange (peeled, quartered & sliced crosswise)
- ✓ 4 fresh mint leaves (thinly sliced)

Method:
- Mix honey and yogurt together and pour the mixture over orange slices and spread mint on top.

- A very nutritional easy to make recipe with the nutritional value of 171 calories, 34 g carbohydrates, and 11g proteins.

Recipe 03: Chocolate Ganache Sandwiches

Ingredients:
- ✓ 1 12-ounce bag semisweet chocolate chips
- ✓ 2 cups heavy cream
- ✓ 2-9-ounce boxes Nabisco Famous Chocolate Wafers

Method:

- Take a pan add chocolate chip to it, now heat it on medium flame by adding heavy cream to it.

- Remove from heat and place it in the refrigerator to chill.

- When the chocolate cream has been made, take two wafers and fill them with this chocolate cream and add few tablespoons of ganache as well.

- If you like stiffness in the wafer then make it few minutes before the occasion and if you like the soft wafer, then make the dish a day before. Wafers absorb the cream, leaving the sweet dish soft and creamy cakelike dessert.

Recipe 04: No-Bake Chocolate-Oatmeal Cookies

Ingredients:
- ✓ 2 cups quick-cooking oats (uncooked)
- ✓ 2/3 cup peanut butter
- ✓ 1 (3 1/2-ounce) can flaked coconut

- ✓ ¼ Cup Cocoa
- ✓ 1 tsp. vanilla extract
- ✓ 2 cups sugar
- ✓ ½ cup milk
- ✓ 1/4 cup butter (or margarine)

Method:
- In a bowl add peanut butter, oats, coconut, cocoa, and vanilla and mix well. Set aside for a while

- Take a saucepan and add sugar, milk, and butter to it and bring it to boil. Now cook it for a minute and stir constantly. Add oat mixture to it and stir again to mix well.

- Place on the baking sheet and allow it cool.

- Once cool, serve it.

Recipe 05: Royal Rum Balls

Ingredients:
- ✓ 2 cups gingersnap crumbs

- ✓ 2 cups chocolate wafer crumbs

- ✓ 1 1/2 cups sifted powdered sugar

- ✓ 1 cup flaked coconut

- ✓ 1 cup ground pecans (toasted)

- ✓ 1/3 cup pitted dates (chopped)

- ✓ 1/3 cup dark rum

- ✓ 3 tbsp. light corn syrup

- ✓ 2 tbsp. butter or margarine, melted

- ✓ 1 tsp. vanilla extract

- ✓ Powdered sugar

Method:
- In a food processor, add the first 6 ingredients and blend well. Now add in the next 3 ingredients as well and mix until they bind well together.

- Take out the mixture and shape them into balls in sugar or gingersnap crumbs. Repeat the rolling procedure.

- Refrigerate them to stiff the binding more and serve.

Recipe 06: Rocky Road Brownies

Ingredients:
- ✓ 1/2 cup butter (1/4 lb.)

- ✓ 3 ounces unsweetened chocolate (chopped)

- ✓ 1 1/3 cups sugar

- ✓ 2 large eggs

- ✓ 1 tsp. vanilla

- ✓ 1/2 cup all-purpose flour

- ✓ 1 cup miniature marshmallows

- ✓ ½ cup walnuts (chopped)

Method:
- Take a pan and heat it on low flame. Add butter and chocolate to it and stir until it melts well. Remove it from the

heat and add into it sugar, vanilla, eggs, flour, and marshmallows and blend it well.

- In a baking pan, spread the batter and sprinkle walnuts on the top. Bake the batter for 30-35 minutes at a 350 degree.

- To ensure its wellness, insert a fork or a knife in the brownie. If it's dry, it means it well made inside. Remove from the oven and cool it.

- Once it's cool, cut it into pieces of your choice and serve.

- If you like the chill desert then refrigerate it before consuming but make sure to cover it.

Recipe 07: 5-Ingredient Sugar Cookies

Ingredients:
- ✓ 1/2 cup butter (softened)

- ✓ 3 cups powdered sugar (divided)

- ✓ 1 large egg

- ✓ 1 1/2 teaspoons vanilla extract
- ✓ 1 1/2 cups all-purpose flour
- ✓ Parchment paper
- ✓ White nonpareils

Method:

- In the electrical beater bowl, beat butter and sugar at the medium speed. Now add egg and vanilla and beat for 30 seconds. Now add flour and beat again until it combines well.

- Place the dough on the parchment paper and make a good dough. Flatten the dough and with the help of various shaped cutters, cut them into different shapes.

- Grease the baking tray with flour and place the cookies on it. Make sure to preheat the oven to 375 degrees.

- Bake the cookies in batches for around 10 minutes till they get a good golden color.

- Remove from the oven and set aside to cool for 30 minutes.

- Make a mixture of sugar in water and dip the cookies in the glaze, sprinkle it with nonpareils and set aside for an hour.

Recipe 08: Frozen Yogurt covered Blueberries

Ingredients:
- ✓ 1/2 cup Plain, Nonfat Greek Yogurt

- ✓ 40 drops Stevia Extract

- ✓ 1/3 cup Blueberries (fresh (rinsed, dried and picked over)

Method:
- In a small bowl add yogurt and stir it either in stevia or honey, it depends on your choice.

- Take blueberries, insert the toothpick into them and dip them in yogurt and push it with another toothpick. Do this procedure with all the berries and put the pan in the freezer for two hours.

- Blueberries can be stored well by placing them in the sandwich bag and freezing.

Recipe 09: Strawberry Cheesecake

Ingredients:
- ✓ 1/2 cup cream cheese (fat-free)
- ✓ 2 tbsp. Coconut Palm Sugar
- ✓ ½ cup low-fat Greek yogurt
- ✓ 2 tsp. lemon juice (freshly squeezed)
- ✓ ¼ cup strawberry
- ✓ 1/3 cup whole almonds
- ✓ 4 dates
- ✓ 8 Mini Dessert Dishes, 3-4 ounces

Method:
- Take a bowl, add sugar, cream cheese, yogurt, and lemon juice to it. Make a fine texture by the help of the electric beater. Beat the mixture for 3 minutes and then refrigerate it.

- In a bowl add strawberries and in the food processor add almonds and chop them and into it add dates and pulse. Make sure not to make to make the mixture very fine.

- Divide the mixture in the dessert serving bowls or dishes and top each with ½ cheesecake and yogurt batter. Add the strawberry mixture to it and refrigerate it for 3 hours minimum.

- For the best result make it before time and place it in the freezer to be used later.

Recipe 10: No-Bake Recipe: Coconut Snowballs

Ingredients:
- ✓ 1 ¾ cups unsweetened shredded coconut (divided)

- ✓ 2 tsp. coconut oil (melted)

- ✓ 3 tbsp. maple syrup

- ✓ 2 tbsp. coconut milk (unsweetened)

- ✓ ½ tsp. vanilla extract

✓ ½ tsp. ground cinnamon

✓ 1/8 tsp. sea salt

Method:
- In a food processor place 1 cup of shredded coconut along with coconut oil and process it on high speed. Keep on mixing until a fine texture is made. The texture should be paste-like and no less, but also make sure it does not become very smooth like the butter.

- In a bowl add coconut milk, vanilla, maple syrup, and cinnamon, salt and process it until it combines well. To the mixture, add ½ cup of pulse, 2 tablespoons of coconut (shredded) and pulse to combine it well.

- When the mixture is well made, shape them into balls and coat it with the remaining leftover shredded coconut and refrigerate it for at least an hour before serving.

- This sweet dish can be used for up to 5 days if it's preserved well in the refrigerator.

- Before eating make sure to set it at room temperature and then enjoy!

Conclusion:

Clean eating is not a luxury or a trend to follow, but it's a necessity of today's time, to stay healthy and in shape. Clean eating is nothing but a "un-fad" diet which results in a healthy lifestyle. Eating healthy is a necessity because the artificially processed food items are high in sodium, fats, and calories, which is not good for the body in the long run.

Today majority of us are prone to heart disease, liver and kidney failures, least immunity levels and what not just because we have stopped making an effort in eating clean food. Processed food might taste good to the tongue because of the high spices or strong artificial flavors, but they leave drastic impacts on the body.

A healthy diet is rich in healthy fats, greater content of water, lean proteins and carbohydrates. Clean eating is merely not a diet but a lifestyle to run all your life. It does take time to settle in for the change but when the change such a worth, then why not change?

Clean eating makes you feel better by eating simple meals with the combinations of vegetable and fruits. The best thing about vegetables and fruits is it does not make you feel acidic or too much full leading to gastric troubles. You are not only exempted from the gastric troubles, but also from heart disease, liver kidney failure and various other disease resulting to aging before time. Healthy foods promote cell growth due to which your skin, nails, hair and weight remains healthy and fresh. Vegetable and fruits are the natural curers for small and big diseases and effect more than the artificial supplements.

Clean eating enables you to maintain a healthy weight naturally for natural foods does not make your belly hang loosely giving you an untidy look. The fibers you gain from vegetables make you lose weight naturally without any side effect at all. For all those who doubt clean eating or are feeling lazy to follow it should know that clean eating builds a better immune system. According to the latest research doctors have proven that natural diet cures the illness more than the medicines. Fruits aid as the natural healer to the body like apples, banana, mango, watermelon, kiwi, and oranges. It keeps the immune system healthy and kills the bacteria prevailing in the body.

This book encloses all the minute details of how to acquire the natural eating habits and make it a lifestyle. One might would never get bore reading this e-book because it contains such variety of recipes that it satisfies all types of people. Some like more of heavy meals while some prefer lighter ones. This book has a variety and contains various recipes for breakfast, lunch, dinner as well as desserts, making sure no meal is left unturned when it comes to the healthy cooking.

Never think that your budget would crash buying all these things every week or your routine would get more hectic cooking all day. Think broadly and evaluate the benefits and side effects of the artificial food items you consume each day. Do not risk your health for few dollars, instead invest in your health and lead a long healthy life. Clean eating not only keeps you healthy but also provides a soothing effect to your nervous system, providing a sound sleep.

When our immune system stays balance, our sleep gets good, heart beat gets controlled, diseases being eradicated from the body without medicines, skin and hair getting more beautiful, no bloating and gastric problems, then what else do we need to know more to avail clean eating?

Start following the tips and instructions and transform your artificial lifestyle into a healthy one. Stay healthy, fresh, sleep well and lead a long life with all zest and zeal.

54772334R00044

Made in the USA
Lexington, KY
27 August 2016